SYMPHONIC REPERTOIRE for KEYBOARD PERCUSSION

*A Detailed Analysis of
the Major Orchestral Keyboard Percussion Repertoire*

❧❧

Jack Van Geem

Edited by Anthony J. Cirone

MM

Published by
Meredith Music Publications
a division of G.W. Music, Inc.
4899 Lerch Creek Ct., Galesville, MD 20765
http://www.meredithmusic.com

The publisher wishes to extend thanks to the following manufacturers for providing instrument photographs:
Fall Creek Marimbas: Orchestra Bells
Coe Percussion: Xylophone

International Standard Book Number: 978-1-57463-089-3
Printed and bound in U.S.A.

Contents

Foreword

Music making is much more than transferring notes from the written page to an instrument—it is understanding the explicit and implicit character of those notes. Composers include explicit information in order to help the musician comprehend their musical vision. However, the symbols they use, articulation, phrasing, dynamic control, and expressive directions such as, *morendo, cantabile, maestoso*, etc., are only an approximation of complicated musical gestures. **It is important that we, as musicians, interpret what was intended by these symbols, which, in turn, gives us a deeper sense of music making.**

There is also much implicit information we can acquire by understanding such elements as: structure of notes, character of meter, and rhythmic complexities.

A true musician is the composer's greatest ally because he or she possesses the technical skill for mastering the notes and developing an intimate relationship with the music and, therefore, providing the greatest insight into a composition's potential—maybe even more than the composer had envisioned!

Every musician develops an individual "style" when interpreting music. This style has usually been cultivated in a number of ways by teachers, colleagues, and conductors within a musical community—and in the practice room where we learn to recognize musical elements that resonate with our personalities.

This book is an attempt to present a personal sense of style that might serve as a guide to help others develop their own musical personalities. Since the literature is vast and growing every year, a compendium of musical excerpts is all but impossible; however, I have listed many clear examples of important musical tools I have found useful in my career. That is the purpose of this book. I hope to share the importance of voicing, understanding composer's symbolic instructions, simplifying stickings, developing accuracy, creating musical phrases and searching out implicit dynamics. I have also added some "nuts- and-bolts" suggestions regarding auditions and performance practices.

It is my hope that these tools will provide you with insights for developing style and will increase your depth of musical understanding as you study the concepts used in these musical examples.

As I mentioned, the musical community within which we grow is a large part of our development and I certainly have benefited from a particularly rich one. I've had the joyous experience of playing and learning in a section filled with wonderful, talented, and generous musicians. Their feedback and support have helped me become the musician I am. Lloyd Davis, Peggy Luchessi, Tom Hemphill, Raymond Froelich, Trey Wyatt, Dave Herbert, and, of course, Tony Cirone, have enriched my life professionally and personally in a way the greatest expression of gratitude could never repay. So I will close with a simple, affectionate … thank you to all!

Jack Van Geem

MAGIC FLUTE

Wolfgang Amadeus Mozart

Overture

Orchestra Bells

There has been quite a bit of discussion and speculation about the selection of mallets to use for this excerpt. This music was written for a keyboard Glockenspiel (Jeu de Timbres), similar to a celesta, which is not used today. **Attempting to make it easier to play softly by using small-headed mallets compromise the true sound of the instruments and diminish the ability to produce a musical performance by shrinking the dynamic range.** I use a pair of large hard plastic mallets to get a warm, full sound.

There are no dynamics marked in the music. **I suggest playing at a *mf* level. The entire excerpt is played one octave lower than written.**

1. <u>Opening Phrase</u>

There are actually two voices operating here. A lower melodic voice and an upper harmonic voice. The melodic voice ends on the downbeats and the harmonic voice follows on the 2nd and 3rd beats. Notice how the two voices combine in the 5th measure and the 8th and 9th measures (see brackets). This pattern continues throughout the excerpt. **Do not accent the final notes of the phrases.** Below is a more musical approach to phrasing this music:

2. Opening Phrase:

There are a number of options in sticking this music. **I use doubles to avoid crossing.**
This keeps the bars directly under your hands making it easier to strike the correct
notes and maintain the delicacy of the phrasing.

3. High D:

**Take a little time (*poco rallentando*) as you approach the high Ds (and the final
notes of the excerpt).** Below is the sticking I suggest:

„Die Zauberflöte"

GLOCKENSPIEL.

Ouverture tacet.

ACT I.

N° 1–7 tacet.

W. A. Mozart, Werk 620

DON JUAN

Richard Strauss

Glockenspiel (mit Klaviatur.)

This excerpt is one of a number of compositions that present an interesting challenge because they are written for an instrument that is no longer used. Wagner, Strauss and Mahler are among the composers that wrote for this instrument. It was a keyboard instrument that had very heavy bars which were struck with small hammers with whale bone shafts. The sound was powerful and the range of the instrument was much larger than the standard set of orchestra bells. Players today have to deal with deciding which octaves best fit these excerpts.

I suggest using a pair of large brass mallets for much of this excerpt instead of the more common small-headed brass beaters. However, hard plastic mallets should still be used when a warmer, gentler sound is desired. **The entire piece (with one exception) is played one octave lower than written.**

1. First and Third Measures of Letter A, One Measure before Letter B and Letter B:
    Play these measures with large brass mallets. The high E at Letter B should also have an accent.

2. Four Measures before Letter D:
    Play this section with hard plastic mallets. This *tremolo* should have a relaxed, unhurried comfortable sound. Begin at a *pp* level and make the *diminuendo* as indicated, however, add a slight *crescendo* up to a *p* level for the five solo notes speeding up the tremolo slightly as you *crescendo*. **Make a slight lift between the end of the *crescendo* and the next entrance to be sure the first of the five notes is heard as part of the solo and not the end of the *tremolo*.** Below is a more accurate notation of this entrance:

3. Four Measures before Letter K:
    Return to brass mallets here. I play this section in octaves (but "ghost" the bottom octave) to give a little more substance to the sound.

4. Eight Measures before Letter Q:
    I use plastic mallets for this solo before Letter Q. This section should be played with an aggressive character. Play the 16th notes a bit less to be sure they don't compete with the B and E. Muffle the F# and G# triplet notes to help with the *diminuendo*.

5. Letter Q:
   Observe the note values at Letter Q by muffling each note.

6. Five Measures before Letter S:
   Play this measure with brass mallets.

7. Four Measures before Letter U:
   Add the upper octave at Letter U to intensify the *crescendo*.

8. Two Measures before Letter Y:
   Add octaves on the G#, A, A# and B starting in the second measure before Letter Y. Notice the accents on the Ab pick-up notes, they are difficult to see in the part.

9. Letter Aa:
   Play this passage as written (not one octave lower) and add octaves in the third measure after Letter Aa. This is for a change of color. **I use plastic mallets for this passage.**

10. Rest of the Movement:
    I use brass mallets for the remainder of the movement. Two suggestions for the final ascending B Major arpeggio; dampen each note as the following note is played and play the final B above the F#.

DON JUAN.

Glockenspiel.
(mit Klaviatur.)

Richard Strauss, Op. 20.

+) Bei gewöhnlichem Glockenspiel ist hier nur ein Viertel e zu spielen und die tremolos zu pausiren.

EDWIN F. KALMUS

Glockenspiel.

SORCERER'S APPRENTICE

Paul Dukas

Glockenspiel

It is important to think of this entire piece as though it was written in 9/8. Most of the time, conductors will conduct this work with a beating pattern of three beats over three measures instead of one beat to a measure as written. The expanded measures particularly help to give a more controlled and effective *crescendo* in the solo at four measures after Number 17 since you can use the 9/8 downbeats to gauge the pace of the *crescendo*. This also provides a larger meter structure to show phrasing details.

For example, the downbeat at three measures before Number 19 is a bit stronger than the next measure, and the 16th notes can be played much lighter and then lead into the next big downbeat. This approach creates a more effective, musical phrase throughout the measures, without losing any intensity. It is also easier to play the 16th notes more accurately when the dynamic is relaxed a bit. I have added a *ff* to the fourth measure after Number 19 which is not in the part, but is a good target dynamic (don't overplay!)

A brief note about the grace notes throughout the piece, they should be performed in a crisp manner and should not sound like 16th notes. The grace notes should also be softer than the main notes and finally they should all be played in a consistent manner.

1. <u>Four Measures after Number 17 to Four Measures after Number 19:</u>
   Below is the sticking I suggest for this passage:

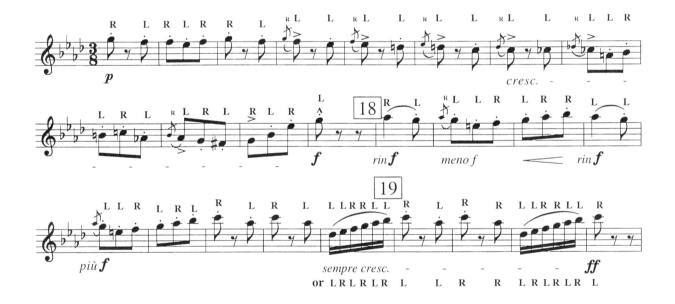

2. Number 18:

The *rin f* indication comes from *rinforzando* which is similar to *sforzando* and means to reinforce the sound at that moment. Again, remember to play with a 9/8 "feel" to lighten up what could be a heavy moment. In some scores, the *rin f* indication is actually written as *rfz*. Reduce the second measure after Number 18 to a *meno f* and then *crescendo* into the next *rin f*.

3. Number 22 to Number 24:

The measures from Number 22 to Number 24 have many issues. **I suggest learning the section on a marimba or xylophone.** Not only is it easier on the ears, but it allows us to hear the right notes from the wrong notes. I find many students cannot hear wrong notes among the Glockenspiel's overtones. Also, practice playing all five notes in a single motion thereby creating a smooth phrase for each group.

Continue the 9/8 "feel" with a clear emphasis on the first note of each group. Pay close attention to this detail when the phrase turns around in the third, sixth, and eighth measures after Number 23. Give a full rhythmical value to the 8th note at the end of each group as you prepare to start the next one. It can be easy to make these notes sound like quintuplets. **The sticking for the descending runs is: RRLRL; all ascending runs are: LRLRL.** The final run starts on the left hand.

4. Three Measures before Number 24:

Provide some dynamic profile to the trill by using a reverse hairpin. Then add a slight lift before the grace notes so they sound separate from the trill. Finish the excerpt by dampening the G, Ab and Bb after striking the final A.

5. Below is the sticking and accents I use for the two passages after Number 52:

L'Apprenti Sorcier
Scherzo

(D'après une ballade de Gœthe)

PAUL DUKAS

A. Durand & Fils, Editeurs   D. & F. 5292   Paris, 4, Place de la Madeleine.

GLOKENSPIEL

SYMPHONY No. 5

Gustav Mahler

Glockenspiel

This is another example of the challenge in matching contemporary instruments to the power and range of instruments used at the time of Wagner, Strauss and Mahler.

Use large-headed brass mallets. Choose comfortable and appropriate sized mallets so they do not overwhelm the instrument. Some orchestra bells can be more easily overplayed than others.

For those orchestra bells that have an extended range up to high E, there will not be any transposition problems. I will give alternate instructions for playing these excerpts on the normal 2 1/2 octave instrument.

II - 3. Scherzo

1. The Fourth Measure and Four Measures after Number 17:
This Scherzo has a very strong downbeat feel throughout the movement. This should be clearly heard in the phrasing. Specifically in the fourth measure of the movement and four after Number 17, the D and F# double stop must have the most presence.

2. One Measure before Number 3:
This section can be played as written—beginning on the top F# of the instrument. **I play this section using one mallet while muffling each note with the other hand as the following note is struck**—stick dampening technique without the stick.

If there is no high D on the instrument at six measures after Number 3, play the D down one octave. Strike the D a bit softer than the following B to help minimize the break in the descending line.

At eight measures after Number 3, aim for the F#, the only downbeat, making it the center of a slight hairpin *crescendo*. The F# is missing on the eighth measure after Number 3 in some editions. If you look closely at the actual part, you can tell it has been written in.

3. <u>Fifteen Measures after Number 15</u>:
   The glockenspiel plays very dramatic F naturals with the characteristic 3/4 rhythm. **I perform this section with one hand for a more consistent and focused sound.** However, the rhythm is more important than the sound and if the notes become sluggish using one mallet, then I suggest using two mallets. Again, emphasize the downbeats.

4. <u>Number 18</u>:
   I play Number 18 a bit different than at Number 3 as indicated below. Notice that Mahler has added the key signature this time.

   Continue to hold two mallets and play the B natural before Number 19 as a double stop (octaves). Mahler frequently writes a single glockenspiel note at important places in the music. Many times this note must compete with the power of the entire orchestra, so I seldom play them as single notes.

   However, when adding the octave, be sure the written note dominates the sound. Many times, I will play the added octave with a hard plastic mallet and the written note with a brass mallet. The plastic mallet "warms" up the sound so it is more sensed than heard. This is a good spot to try this effect.

5. <u>Eighteen Measures after Number 19</u>:
   The printed triangle note at eighteen measures after Number 19 is an error. There is no note at this spot in the score.

6. <u>One Measure after Number 20</u>:

At one measure after Number 20, the downbeats, F natural and C#, on the second and third measures are the interesting notes. Stress these notes and lay off the notes on the second beat of the measures. There is no need for muffling here. There is no dynamic marking at Number 20, in some editions it is marked as a *ff*, however save something for other more dramatic moments such as the octaves.

Add a *crescendo* in the second measure of Number 20 and continue the *crescendo* to the 8th note pickups into the octaves. This is an important gesture and works best without displacing any of the octaves. Therefore, if your instrument does not have an extended range, play this entire section down one octave beginning in the fifth measure after Number 20.

Below is a more accurate notation for this section without an extended range on the glockenspiel:

7. <u>Number 27</u>:

At Number 27, we have reached the most intense moment of the movement and although the dynamic does not indicate this, it is loud! Add a *crescendo* from the first note and pace it well until the end of the passage. Drop off a bit on the second beats of measures 2, 3, and 4. **I begin to add octaves six measures after Number 27 to add to the power of the music.** At nine measures after Number 27, Mahler adds octaves which are out of the range of a Glockenspiel. When the music goes beyond the range of the instrument, leave out the top notes, but emphasize the lower notes. **Do not play this section down an octave because is loses its intensity and brilliance if played in the lower octave.**

Below is a more accurate notation:

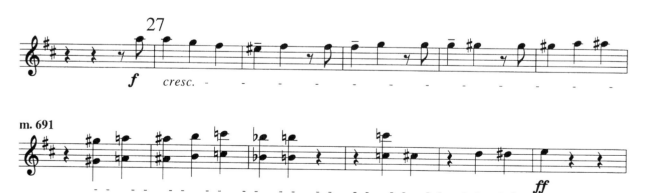

Kleine Trommel, Tamtam, Triangel, Glockenspiel & Holzklapper.

II.
3. Scherzo.

LA MER

Claude Debussy

Glockenspiel

The use of a celesta or glockenspiel is indicated in the part. This is another opportunity to show the advantage the glockenspiel has for producing a greater variety of colors. **This movement is played as written with the exception of Number 21 and four measures from the end which must be played one octave lower than written.**

II. Jeux de vagues

1. Measures Two and Four:
   Although these four notes have *staccato* markings, they are not played short. Debussy uses the *staccato* to indicate articulation and not whether to sustain the notes. Do not muffle the sound of these four notes.

2. Number 16 to Number 18:
   I suggest hard plastic mallets for this section. Phrase the 3/8 pulse with slight accents on the first high C and the following downbeats from one measure after Number 16 to five measures after Number 16. At four measures before Number 17, pulse the bottom A# and B to show the duple phrase.

3. Number 18:
   To create the correct character for this part, practice it without the triplet 32nd note. Then add the 32nd note with a grace-note feeling.

4. Number 21 to Number 22:
   This section must be played down one octave lower than written. I switch to two pairs of softer mallets at Number 21—of these two pairs, one is softer than the other. The instrument makes it difficult to produce the *diminuendo* because as you descend the notes speak more easily. With number one as the top mallet, hold the harder mallets as 1 and 3 and the softer mallets as 2 and 4. Then use a 1, 3, 2, 4 sticking. In this way, the softer beaters will help to "show" the *diminuendo*. Listen to the harp for rhythmic accuracy. Below shows how the two instruments interact:

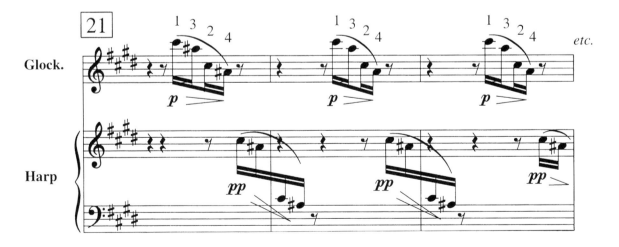

5. <u>Four Measures after Number 25:</u>
   Return to the hard plastic mallets at four measures after Number 25 and exaggerate the two-note phrase groups of beats one and two (but not on beat three) by playing the first notes slightly louder. For auditions, it's nice to add a slight *rallentando* at the end of this phrase. During actual performances, this must be coordinated with the oboe player.

   Notice the subtle *crescendo, decrescendo* and dynamic additions below which shape this beautiful phrase. Let the final note sustain.

6. <u>Two Measures before Number 32:</u>
   I suggest brass mallets for this section and my preferred sticking is shown below. Notice the sextuplet indication (6) which is not in the original part, but is technically correct. Also there are dynamics added to indicate the composer's intent.

7. <u>Number 33 to number 34:</u>
   I play this just as it appears, with a *sub. pp* after the first *crescendo*. The second entrance is a *poco cresc.* to a *mp*.

8. <u>Four Measures before the End of the Movement:</u>
   Play this measure one octave lower than written. Use the four softer mallets here, take your time and enjoy the moment. I suggest a 4, 2, 3, 1 sticking pattern, with the harder mallets as 4 and 2 and the softer mallets as 3 and 1.

III. Dialogue du vent et de la mer

   This entire movement should be played down one octave lower than written.

7. <u>Nine Measures after Number 55 to Eight Measures before Number 56:</u>
   Use slightly warmer sounding plastic mallets for this solo. Observe the *legato* and *staccato* phrase markings by playing the *staccato* notes softer.

   The third beat in the second measure and the first beat in the third measure do not have a *tenuto* marking. I find it more interesting to play it without adding *tenuto* markings.

8. <u>Ten Measures before Number 56:</u>
   In the second half of this phrase, save the softest dynamic for the last two measures, ten measures before Number 56, to trick the ear into hearing the effect of the ties. For auditions, take a bit of time ending the phrase and add a slight *decrescendo.*

9. <u>Five Measures after Number 58 to Three Measures after Number 59:</u>
   I use the following sticking for these last two phrases. The doubles help keep the arms quiet and make it easier to play the *diminuendo.* Add *diminuendos* to the second entrance at Number 59.

LA MER

Trois esquisses symphoniques pour orchestre

CLAUDE DEBUSSY

GLOCKENSPIEL ou CELESTA

N° 1.— De l'aube à midi sur la mer: TACET

N° 2.— Jeux de vagues

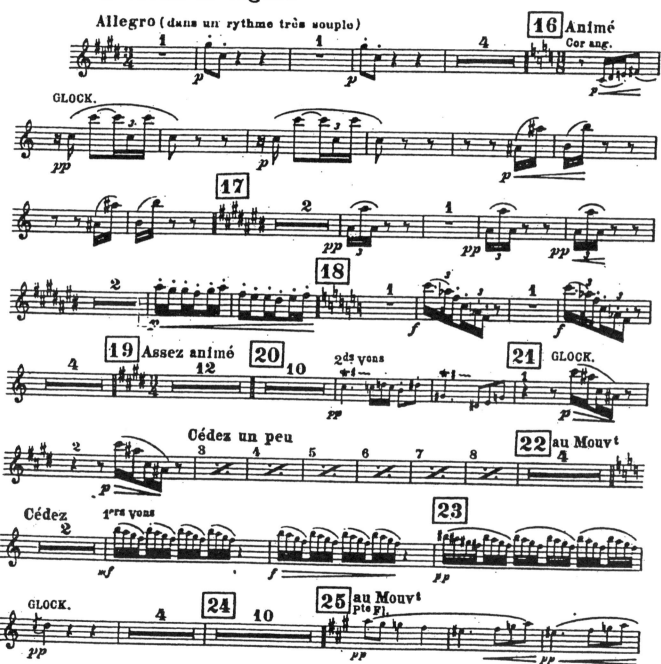

EDWIN F. KALMUS, Publisher of Music, New York 1, N. Y.

GLOCKENSPIEL

GLOCKENSPIEL

N° 3 _ Dialogue du vent et de la mer

PINES OF ROME

Ottorino Respighi

Campanelli

This entire part should be played one octave lower than written.

1. Opening:
   This opening music should be played with as big and round a sound as possible.
   Some manufacturers make a mallet designed to enhance the fundamentals of the bar.
   These would work well here. Create as much musical bravado as possible. Make a
   diminuendo during the descending lines and a *crescendo* during the ascending lines.
   Phrase as though this was written in 3/4 as indicated below by the slurs.

2. Number 2:
   Do not change the pulse at the 3/8 measure (the 8th notes are not equal). The
   downbeats stay the same ($2/8 = 3/8$). Once in the 3/8 time, keep a strong pulse on the
   first beat of each measure in the moving passages.

3. Seven Measures after Number 2:
   **It is necessary to switch to three mallets at this spot. I add the third mallet
   during the 9 measure rest after Number 1. I suggest hard plastic mallets.**

   The goal of sticking throughout this piece is to minimize awkward arm movements
   that make it difficult to control dynamics. For example, try the following sticking for
   this passage beginning at seven measures after Number 2. Notice the comfortable
   arm movement and how much easier it is to find the right notes.

   A small musical issue about this passage is that the articulation implies a strong pulse
   on each measure. So use the downbeats to gauge the *crescendo* with the loudest note
   being the top accented D and not the following A.

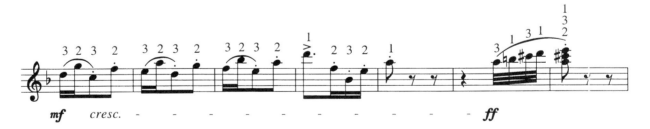

4. <u>Number 3 to Seven Measures after Number 4</u>:
   The 32nd notes and triplet 32nd notes between Number 3 and seven measures after Number 4 should all be played as ornaments. They should never compete with the downbeats for attention. Play them lightly. Once you arrive at the trill, drop the dynamic down to a *mf* and delay the *crescendo* until the final four measures.

5. <u>Seven Measures after Number 8</u>:
   From here to the end it appears only three mallets are necessary, but I find it easier to play this section holding four mallets. Below is the sticking I use for this section:

6. <u>Thirteen Measures after Number 8</u>:
   Think of this section in two-measure units. The bottom A is louder than the top A.

7. <u>Eight Measures before Number 9</u>:
   Below is the sticking I suggest for this section:

8. <u>Number 9</u>:
   The trills at Number 9 can be a technical as well as a musical problem. In the course of the *stringendo,* the notes tend to sound heavy and cumbersome.

   The trill should slightly decay after the initial attack. **Use only four strokes per trill, but play them faster than the following 16th notes so there is a space after the trill.** As you accelerate, the space gets shorter. This approach avoids the need of an excessive amount of strokes in the trill. The combination of all the above comments results in making it easier to play this section well. More importantly, it produces a light, sparkling charm that marks the entire movement.

O. RESPIGHI

PINI DI ROMA

I. I pini di Villa Borghese

CAMPANELLI

Proprietà G. RICORDI & C., Editori - Stampatori. MILANO.   (Copyright MCMXXV. by G. RICORDI & Co.)
119882 - XXVIII

IL RESTO TACE

PORGY AND BESS*
Overture

George Gershwin

Xylophone

This music from the Overture to the Opera, Porgy and Bess, is related to "ragtime". Do not be baffled by the accents or turn them into a bloodless exercise in specious precision. There should be a lightness to this excerpt and a sense of musical shape as directed by the accents.

It is much easier for the conductor to move the baton four times a measure then for the percussionist to move the mallets sixteen times a measure. Combine this with the sometimes excitable tempos we may experience during any given performance, and we can easily become a victim of an unexpectedly "splashy" tempo. **I choose to play this excerpt hand to hand to avoid becoming that victim!**

One suggestion to increase control and accuracy of hand to hand sticking, is to choose your beating spots and the angle of the mallets carefully. I begin with the right hand on the F#, with the head of the mallet slightly above the left hand on the G#. The right hand would be the upper beating spot and the left hand the lower beating spot. I prefer the sound slightly off center and it helps with the sticking issues.

The angle of the mallets is also important (90 degrees or more). This allows the mallets to move past each other without having to lift one mallet up and away from the field of play.

1. <u>Measures 7, 12, 13, 14 and 16 after the Allegro con brio:</u>
   There are three double strokes and one note played on the end of the bar.
   Everything else is played on the top or bottom center spots of the bars. Below is the sticking I suggest:

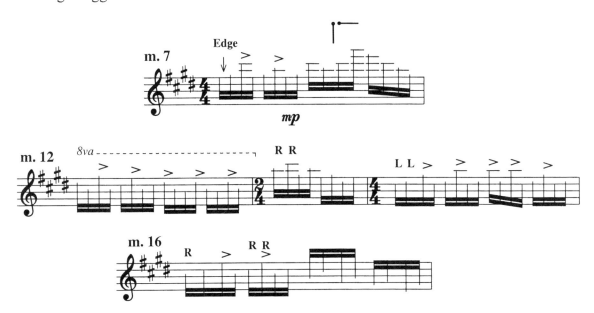

2. <u>See Asterisks below:</u>

*a. This is the first example where many misses or near misses occur. The secret is to separate the shafts by a little more than 90 degrees as these notes are being played. Go straight to each note using the center of the bars and miraculously everything lands safely.

*b. On the second of these examples, a slight turn of the body will switch the shaft angle so you can exit the passage more easily.

3. <u>Entire Passage:</u>

Finally, a few details to focus on a better musical performance. **Notice the additional accent on the downbeat of 15 measures after the Allegro. Note the suggested hairpin** *crescendos* **and** *decrescendos* **and subtle dynamic changes.**

PORGY AND BESS
Overture

Xylophone

By George Gershwin

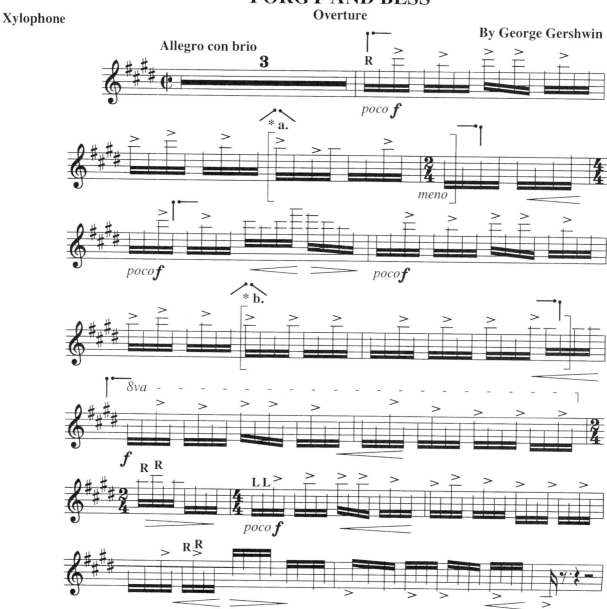

MUSIC FOR STRINGS, PERCUSSION AND CELESTE

Béla Bartok

Xylophone

Movement III

1. Measure Two:
   The *rubato* indication in the second measure is not meant to take liberties with the pulse, but rather with the rhythm. It should feel like an *accelerando* up to the downbeat of the third measure. Then slow down as written through Number 5. **The downbeat of measure 3 should not be played as a roll but as 32nd notes that speed up and slow down.** Also, the triplet rhythm before and after the 32nd notes, should not be played as an exact rhythm, but in a way that continues the speeding up and slowing down between measures 2 and 3. Remember all of this is done within a steady pulse.

   I perform this with one hand except for the triplets and 32nd notes—which I alternate beginning with my left hand.

   The other similar spots at Number 17 and Number 80, I also perform with one hand.

   A more modern notation of this effect may look as follows:

Movement IV

2. Measure 173 to Measure 183:
   The most important element in this passage that begins on measure 173, besides the correct notes, is the phrasing. It begins with seven–note phrase groups. Make a slight *diminuendo* into the last note of each group to create a beautiful shape to the phrase.

   The fourth group of notes gets interrupted to begin the group again. Continue the *crescendo* until the G# in the fourth group (m. 180), but at this point it suddenly gets louder to show the tension as the phrasing is interrupted. The phrase ends with two six-note phrase groups; continue the *crescendo* through these two groups.

3. <u>Number 180.</u>

Beginning on the last beat of Number 180, some players double each note by playing 8th notes. This duplicates the celesta part. I suggest alternating strokes starting on the right hand instead of playing double strokes. Notice in the actual part that the G on the fourth beat of one before Number 180 is missing the sharp.

When striking the accidentals, the head of the right-hand mallet should play on the right edge of the bar and the left-hand mallet on the left edge to help keep the sticks from striking each other.

Be aware that not all conductors will approve of playing these notes as double strokes and may want to hear the original notation, so prepare both versions. **If a conductor asks you not to play doubles, your response should be....Yes, Maestro!**

Below is the original excerpt with my stickings, phrases and dynamic changes:

Below is this excerpt with double strokes:

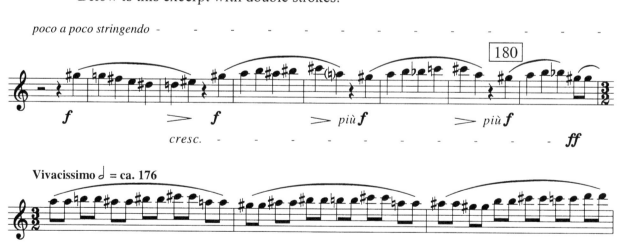

Xylophono

III

Xylophono
IV.

COLAS BREUGNON
Suite from the Opera
Overture

Dmitri Kabalevsky

Xylophone

The main issue with this excerpt is to keep the mallets from running into each other. After years of dealing with double strokes and awkward arm movements that result from leading this excerpt with the right hand, I finally realized this is one of the excerpts that favor a left hand lead. With this is mind, let's look at a few spots in particular.

1. Six Measures after Number Nine:
   The sixth measure after Number Nine is a good place to start. If you stick this measure R, L, R, L, the left mallet on E blocks the right mallet from hitting the D. Similarly, if the right hand strikes the D it blocks the left hand from going to the C#. **Starting on the left hand, with the left-hand mallet parallel to the bars, makes the arm movement much more comfortable.**

2. Number Ten:
   Starting with the left hand on the second beat of measure eleven and using double strokes as in the sticking pattern shown below, makes it easier to start the passage and keeps you from having to switch the hands back and forth between the accidentals.

3. Measures Five, Six and Seven after Number 36:
   Another famous "minefield" of wrong notes is five, six and seven measures after Number 36. Alternating this passage is difficult because the stick angles have to change in each measure. However the note landscape is such that if you begin this passage with the left hand, it allows the notes to proceed in a smooth manner. Try the two stickings below:

4. <u>Number 9 to Number 12 and One before Number 36 to Number 37:</u>
   The musical character should have a lightness despite the *f* and *ff* dynamics. To this end, I have indicated a fairly busy roadmap of hairpins, accents and phrase markings for playing this excerpt. Below is a complete version with stickings and dynamic additions:

COLAS BRUEGNON

XILOFONO OVERTURE D.KABALEVSKY

EDWIN F. KALMUS, Publisher of Music, New York, N. Y.

XILOFONO

XILOFONO

XILOFONO

APPALACHIAN SPRING

Aaron Copland

Xylophone

Let's begin with the accuracy issue first.

a. **The secret is that you cannot strike what you cannot see.** Before practicing this excerpt on the keyboard, be able to play it mentally in your head. By this I mean you should see the actual notes struck on an imaginary keyboard in your head.

b. Pay close attention to the movement of your arms—they should move together. **The arms are responsible for accuracy.**

c. **Relax the dynamic of the left hand so the right hand is clearly heard as the melody note.** This provides a more musical approach to the excerpt.

Copland used the same articulations for the xylophone that he used for the wind players. Unfortunately, we do not have control over the length of our notes, so all of the articulations must be controlled by dynamics. Copland uses the following articulations in the xylophone part from five after Number 48 to four after Number 49: heavy wedge, staccato, accent, tenuto, and accent staccato. **To understand what needs to be accomplished, sing the passage with the specific articulations.** Notice how the notes marked with *legato* have more presence than the *staccato* notes, so lighten up on the *staccato* notes. The heavy wedge is the most dramatic articulation meaning heavy and short.

Since the only control we have over these articulations is dynamic control, the following is a listing of the articulations from a normal stroke to the most dramatic:

1. <u>Five Measures after Number 48 to One Measure before Number 49:</u>
   Below is my musical approach to this passage using the articulations listed above:

2. <u>One Measure before Number 49:</u>

Provide some relief for the repeated notes by using what I call "telephone wire" dynamics. After a strong entrance, add a slight *diminuendo* to the center of the measure and then *crescendo* back up to the next measure. Below is a more accurate indication of this:

Even if the orchestra does not play these measures in this manner, it provides an interesting color change that helps frame the accents.

3. <u>Final Three Measures:</u>

The last group of glockenspiel notes at the end of the piece may be difficult to play together with the harp. This becomes easier if you take the preparatory stroke of the mallet out of the equation. Position the mallet over the bar at the appropriate height for the dynamic level and drop the mallet at the point in the conductor's beat that you and the harpist decide is the NOW!

Appalachian Spring Percussion

Aaron Copland

Percussion

HÁRY JÁNOS SUITE

Zoltan Kodaly

Xylophone

VI – Entrance of the Emperor and his Court

1. <u>Opening:</u>

   The grace notes, that provide such a wonderful character to the opening of the Movement VI, also give the percussionist a wonderful headache. The trick that makes them easier to perform also makes them more musically appropriate. Find the beating spots for all four notes. I begin with my left hand and place the left wrist between the Bb edge and the D middle. The right hand wrist is between the C middle and Eb middle. Practice by striking the bars without moving your arms; just use a sideways motion of the wrists.

   The only arm movement will be the right hand as it moves over to strike the Bb eighth note in the center of the bar before returning to its previous spot. This way the three grace notes and the downbeat feel like one light and easy motion.

   Take care that the single grace notes have a similar lightness. When reversing the sticking in the second and third measures before Number 1, the grace notes should sound the same.

   Below indicates the sticking for the entire passage:

2. <u>Number 7:</u>
    I suggest the following sticking for the passage at Number 7. This works well if you position the shafts at a 90 degree angle allowing the left mallet head to reach past the right.

    Even though the dynamic level is *ff*, the music should have a playful character.

3. <u>One Measure after Number 10 to the End.</u>
    I use the following sticking for the inverted mordant after Number 10, which should begin on the Bb and not the C.

    I prefer a double turn (Bb, C, Bb, C, Bb) for a stronger presence. The Bb's are the featured notes in these measures.

    Below is the sticking for this section:

VI
A CSÁSZÁRI UDVAR BEVONULÁSA
EINZUG DES KAISERLICHEN HOFES
ENTRANCE OF THE EMPEROR AND HIS COURT

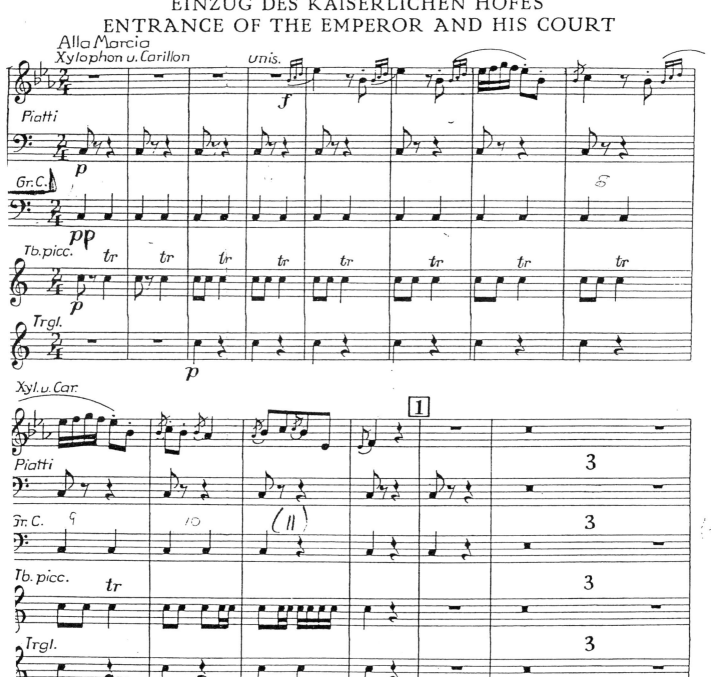

Batteria

Batteria

SYMPHONY No. 3

William Schuman

Xylophone

Part II: d. Toccata

Please note the parenthetical indication at Number 230 that the bottom octave is optional. This would imply that the top octave is the important voice. Pay special attention in keeping the hands balanced so the top octave is more prominent. This also helps the listener to hear the musical quality of the line as well.

Next, position the sticks parallel, so a sideways turning of the wrists can be used to locate the notes. Think of where your wrists would be if you were to play some of the wider intervals holding four mallets. With the wrists in this position, practice moving the mallets back and forth while striking these notes. This requires much less effort and will avoid crushing the downbeats of measures 237 and 238. These notes usually explode, however they should be played in a more delicate manner.

1. Measure 241:
    For the triplet run, beginning measure 241, I suggest the following sticking. It keeps the same mallets over the same notes in all three octaves. **Play this section with a fluid sweep, leading musically to the top note.** This solo is doubled by the Piccolo and Eb Clarinet and both instruments have a slur over the entire phrase, so this is added below for the xylophone part. The dynamic continues from the *mf* level at Number 230.

2. Measure 426 - Final Double Stop of the Work:
    The double stop at measure 426 can be a problem because the bottom note of the double stop is usually overplayed. The figure should end with the top note predominating, the lower note only adding color. It is not an exclamation point.

    The ad libitum indication at the end of the movement refers to the fact that the rest of the piece takes only three players and these final measures take four. The composer may be saying if you need to leave anything out choose between the xylophone and the snare drum.

SYMPHONY NO. 3
By William Schuman

FIREBIRD SUITE (1917 Version)

Igor Stravinsky

Xylophone

1. <u>Number 47 to Number 48</u>:
    There are three important excerpts in this work. The first, from Number 47 to Number 48, is easy to learn as it is based on descending 4th's and chromatic neighboring notes. **To perform this well, a strong sense of "time" is crucial.** Play all the 32nd notes absolutely steady. Continue to feel the 32nd note pulse throughout the rests.

    In each pair of chromatic notes, the first note is more important than the second. Add a subtle accent to the first of each group. To show some musical direction in the repeated notes in the second measure after Number 47, add a slight *crescendo* into the upper A on beat three and finish the excerpt with a *diminuendo.*

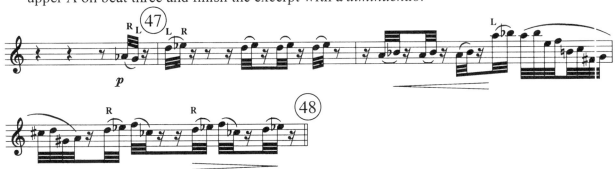

2. <u>Number 129 to Number 133</u>:
    This excerpt is a solo and an important transition into the Allegro feroce at Number 133. What is needed is to generate excitement that justifies the intensity of the succeeding movement. Even though there is no *crescendo* marking in the music, the music demands one to generate this sense of excitement.

    Keep the 16th note rhythm steady. Frequently I hear sudden changes of tempo in the fifth measure after Number 129, for example, and disconcerting changes of pulse during the rests.

    To perform this section in a musically interesting manner, avoid using the same phrase patterns for each group of notes especially during the repeated notes. Create a scheme that shows the intensification of the passage.

    The first four measures of Number 131 and 132 *diminuendo* in the first measure and *crescendo* in the fourth measure. **Repeated notes are never as interesting as changing ones.** The last few measures, beginning at five measures after Number 132 are the loudest, but do not overplay the second and third notes of each group. Continue to show a musical pulse through these measures and *crescendo* to the end.

3. <u>Number 147:</u>
   In this third excerpt, add a slight accent to the second note of each tri-tone group (C#, D# and E, F#). This helps provide the necessary tension in this odd little solo.

4. <u>Number 13 (in the revised 1947 version of the Firebird Suite)</u>
   The Phrygian scale at Number 13 in the 1947 version of the Firebird Suite presents a challenge. There is an ambiguity whether this is, in fact, a *glissando*—as the part indicates—or played as 32nd notes as the score indicates.

   The tempo may dictate how this can be performed. **At slower tempos, the scale may work, however at faster tempos, it may be necessary to play an actual *glissando*.** This may be accomplished by playing a two-octave *glissando* starting on the beat, (starting slow and then speeding up) or a one-octave *glissando* starting on the "an" of one. Prepare all three versions.

   Below shows the piccolo, xylophone and piano parts. Notice the piano part says "*gliss.*" but the xylophone and flute do not, yet all have the same notation. Also, the flute and xylophone have a slur, but the piano does not. These discrepancies all add to the interpretation process and there may not be one correct answer.

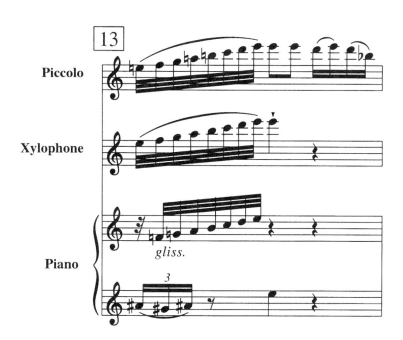

58

Batteria

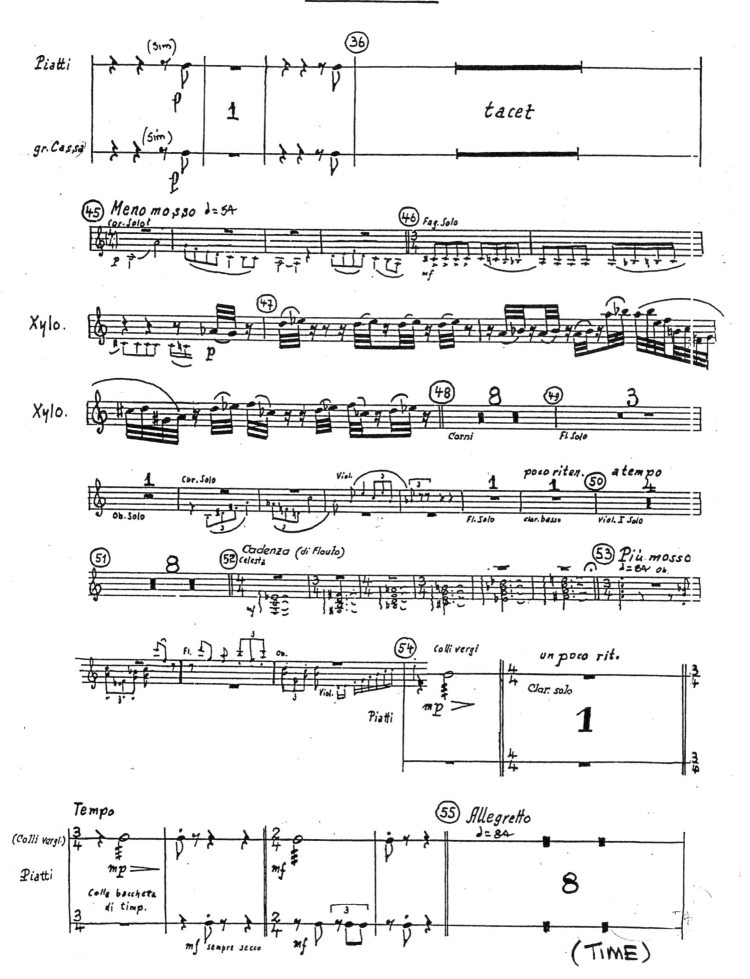

Batteria

60

Ballerina

(Time)

INTRODUCTION

Igor Stravinsky.

TACET

L'OISEAU DE FEU ET SA DANSE
TACET

VARIATION DE L'OISEAU DE FEU
TACET

RONDE DES PRINCESSES
TACET

DANSE INFERNALE DU ROI KASTCHEÏ

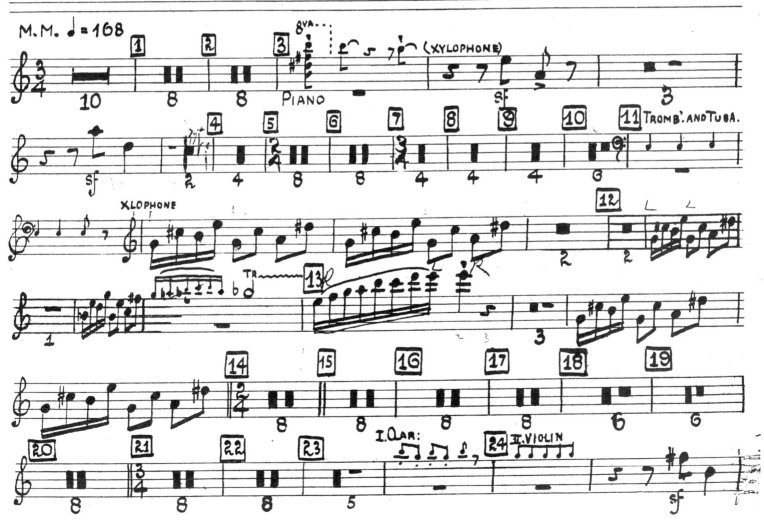

EDWIN F. KALMUS, 51-53 W. 56th Street, New York, N. Y.

POLKA
From the Golden Age Ballet

Dmitri Shostakovich

Xylophone

      One of my teachers told me to think of this excerpt as a "drunken polka". This is a helpful concept. Even a "designated driver" has watched an inebriated dancer reel around a dance floor. Their steps are heavy and don't always land when and where they want. Such is the case with the accented pickup notes which function as a misplaced downbeat.

1. <u>Final Four Measures:</u>
   A word about the question of whether to add an *accelerando* to the last four measures. If you perform this in an audition and you decide to add this *accelerando,* be sure to make it musical. This is not a run-away truck. Keep the pulse clear and push the tempo slightly to the end. The committee must feel you are adding a musical element to the music and not rushing! **Anytime you add something that is not written in the part, it should be subtle.** If you have any doubt, only play what is written.

   Below is my version with added phrasing and dynamics. The sticking is straight forward.

POLKA
(from "THE GOLDEN AGE")
by D. Shostakovich

LES NOCES

Igor Stravinsky

Xylophone

The xylophone part in Les Noces is a rewarding challenge to perform. **A general comment about this part is that almost all of the dynamics are over written.** Stravinsky may have had the sound of a four-row "folk" xylophone in his head. This Russian instrument does not have resonators and the written dynamics may have been appropriate at that time. Russian percussionists would have played this instrument with wooden paddles so rosewood or warm sounding plastic mallets work well.

Another general comment is to pay attention that all of the dyads are voiced so the melodic note is prominent. This provides a cleaner musical profile to the music.

One last comment about playing Stravinsky's music is to observe the inherently vital rhythmic component reflected in his work. Observe the written accents and generally play all downbeats with a strong emphasis. If an accent occurs on several notes and one of them is a downbeat, the downbeat accent should be stronger.

1. <u>Four Measures after Number 42 to One Measures after Number 43:</u>
    In the fourth measure after Number 42, bring out the 8th note line and reinforce the top note of the octaves as indicated. The lower octave provides color and shouldn't detract from the top melody note. The accents in the score and parts do not agree.

    This passage should be played at a *f* level instead of the *ff* indicated in the part.

2. <u>Number 53 to 55 and Number 58 to Two before 59:</u>
    The trills should start in the *f – ff* range and immediately drop down to a *mf*. Then *crescendo* one measure before Number 55 back to *ff*.

3. <u>Four and Seven Measures after Number 55:</u>
    Begin all *glissandi* at a *mf* level and *crescendo* to the ending note. I place my mallet on the B below the C on the first two *glissandi* so when I start to drag the mallet on the keyboard, the first note to sound will be the C and there will not be any added accents.

4. Number 59:

The section that begins at Number 59 shows up on many auditions. **One of the reasons this excerpt is used is because it allows the committee to judge a player's sense of "time".** There is a strong tendency to begin each C scale late. At the beginning of each run, avoid feeling the pulse in the preparatory stroke or the entrance will be late every time. It is necessary to feel the momentum of the C scale before each entrance. Don't approach the scale from a "dead" start. Phrase each scale to the following downbeat with a slight *crescendo*. Do not accent the double stops (A and E) of the scales until three measures after Number 60 when it finally ends on the downbeat. The measure before Number 60 does have a downbeat, but the scale continues until it finally arrives at Number 60.

5. Number 61:

Add a slight *crescendo* into Number 61 and continue this *crescendo* until Number 62 to maintain the intensity; as you can see in the above example.

6. Number 59 to Number 61:

One final note on the section from Number 59 to Number 61 regards the decision whether the music is phrased in 3/4 or 6/8. The time signature indicates 6/8, however, most conductors will conduct this in 3/4. For all practical purposes it does not matter. The xylophone lines should be played as long soaring phrases without any metric pulse except for the important downbeats.

7. Three Measures before Number 62:

Emphasize the downbeats during this passage and bring out the top notes.

8. Number 87:

Add a very big accent on the downbeat of the first and third measures after Number 87 and reduce the dynamic of the tremolo (*ffp*). Then add a *crescendo* a few beats before the next accent. There is a *pause* mark in the score at the end of the second measure of Number 87. Watch the conductor as you make a slight break into next measure.

9. Number 88:

    Sticking and mallet placement are important. Begin the fourth measure after Number 88 with the left hand. The repeated figure of C#, B, E, A is another one of those places where you can position the wrists halfway between the beating spots and use a sideways motion, without moving the arms. Use the center area of the bar for the C# so the left hand does not collide with the right hand.

    Reduce the dynamic level when the repeated figure begins and add a *crescendo* into one beat before Number 89. As with all other tremolos, drop down to *mp* after the *ff* attack at Number 89.

10. Number 89:

    As with the previous tremolo, at Number 87, begin at a lesser dynamic and add a *crescendo* to the last few beats of the roll. Add a lift before the Db which begins the descending line on the "an" of the first beat. This provides better clarity to the musical line. Also add a slight *diminuendo* to the run. Do not add a *crescendo* to the roll at three measures before Number 90.

11. Four Measures after Number 90 to Number 91:
    This time add an accent to the C that begins the *glissando* four measures after Number 90.

12. Number 93 to Number 94:
    Bring out the last octave Eb's in each measure between Number 93 and Number 94.

13.   Two Measures before Number 96 to Number 97:

Phrase the two measures before Number 96 similar to its counterpart at Number 88 by adding the accents to the part. Notice the indication of mallet positions in the fourth measure after Number 96. Begin this passage with the left hand. Strike the Eb in the center of the bar and the Ab at the edge of the bar. As you strike the Db with the right hand, the left hand moves to the center of the bar for the Ab and perpendicular to the bar so the right hand mallet can reach past for the Eb. This allows the right hand to play the Eb and Db with a sideways wrist action and no arm motion.

Bring out the top notes of the double stops in one measure before Number 97.

14.   Number 123 to Number 124:

The final comment is for the double stops at Number 123. The 16th notes must be crisp, which is difficult because of the tempo. Don't try to "over enunciate" this figure. It will sound cumbersome if played too loud. Aim for the second double stop and keep the hands low and relaxed.

DEUXIÈME PARTIE

Quatrième Tableau

Le Repas de Noces

70

OISEAUX EXOTIQUES
(EXOTIC BIRDS)

Olivier Messiaen

Xylophone

There are four general guidelines to keep in mind when preparing for this piece.

a. **Follow all Messiaen's musical instructions.** They are very exact and describe the wonderful character of each transcribed bird call. Basically, a *tenuto* needs more emphasis than ordinary notes, but less than accents. *Staccato* notes should be slightly less than other markings, except when they are coupled with accents which implies a more emphatic emphasis. Pay attention to all dynamic markings, especially the soft ones.

b. **One of the major challenges of this piece is to effectively play all of the musical gestures while covering the entire range of the xylophone.** Striking the low C with the same force as the high C will demonstrate the fact that the high C will need more force to sound balanced with the low C. Use care to balance the dynamics throughout the range.

c. **Another helpful suggestion is that repeated groups of notes, as in measures 7, 8, 9, and 10 after Number 4, should be played softer than non-repeated groups.** The repeated groups should always show a dynamic direction. In this case, drive towards the Ab's with a slight *crescendo.*

d. **A final note about the choice of mallets.** Hard plastic mallets may sound somewhat brittle with the explosive dynamics on the top end of the instrument. Consider a "warmer" plastic sound for most of the piece. An exception might be for the *glissandi* and the section that follows after Number 28 for the soft lines.

I am only dealing with the most commonly requested audition sections. However, remember the above guidelines when preparing the entire work.

1. <u>Number 6:</u>
This passage is a more involved version of Number 4—keep the grace notes on the light side. **The important notes are marked with accents, so be sure the non-accented notes do not compete with them.**

2. <u>Five Measures after Number 6:</u>
Use one hand for the C's at five measures after Number 6 and make certain the high B (in the next measure) is, in fact, the loudest sounding note. In the ninth measure after Number 6, begin at a *mf* level to allow the high C (in the tenth measure) to project. Begin a slight *crescendo* a bit earlier than marked.

3. Thirteen, Fourteen and Fifteen Measures after Number 6:
   Phrase the measures in groups of five notes, beginning each group with an accent.

4. Three Measures before Number 7:
   The *p* on the third beat of the third measure before Number 7 must be very soft—as with all the very quiet dynamics in this piece. The technique I use is to drop the arms quickly from their loud position to produce these soft strokes without using a wrist motion. In other words, do not make two separate motions to make the stroke. By allowing the motion of the arm to strike the bars, and not the wrist motion, you can produce extraordinarily soft attacks. Again, be sure that the final high notes are at least equal to the lower notes.

5. Number 25:
   Instead of playing the *glissandi* in the normal manner by using one mallet in each hand, another possibility is to hold 4 mallets and produce the *glissandi* with both hands playing intervals of a second. This greatly increases the intensity and quality of the *glissandi.*

   Delay the start of the *glissandi* until the end of the third beat and lightly strike the fourth beat with the two mallets of the right hand to create a clear shape and rhythmic presence to the effect. Not all conductors may like this, so be prepared to also play a normal *glissandi* with two mallets and no final note.

6. Number 26 and Number 27:
   At Number 26, the grace notes should be light and be sure the accented notes are clearly heard. The high E's before Number 27 should be very delicate. Beginning on the "an" of 2, the low F's in the second measure after Number 27 must be absolutely *pp*.

7. Three Measures after Number 28:
   Three measures after Number 28 should be played softer than indicated—more like a *mp*.

8. Five Measures before Number 29:
   Continuing to hold four mallets will make playing this passage much easier. Two-mallet sticking is bit cumbersome and not as easy to control the soft dynamics. Using four mallets, reduces the arm motion and gives the passage a quieter and more *legato* feeling. I suggest the following sticking:

Xylophone

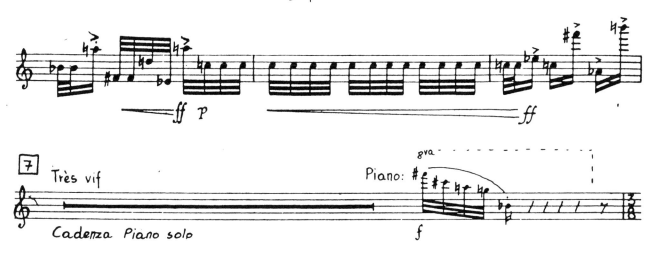

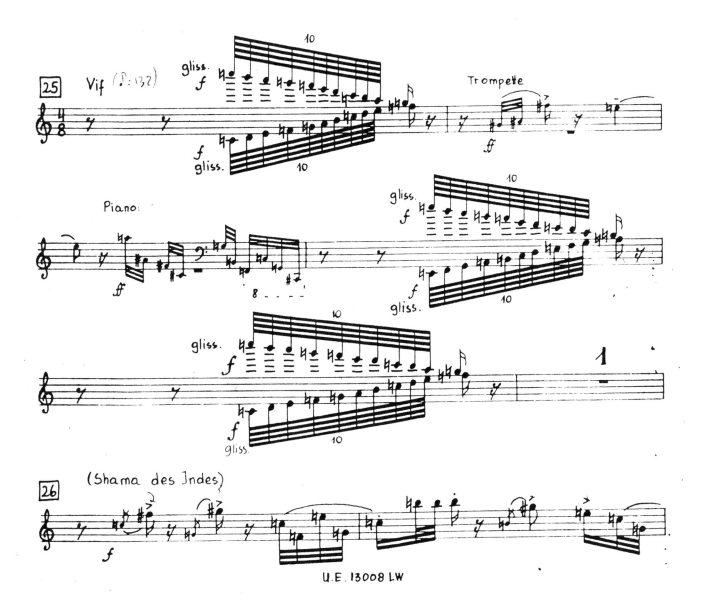

Xylophone

SYMPHONIC DANCES from
WEST SIDE STORY

Leonard Bernstein

Vibraphone

This music is a wonderful part of the percussion literature and is used on many orchestral auditions. It shows a great deal about a player's rhythmic control and musical feel. Both of these elements can be aided or impeded by one's pedaling technique. I have indicated pedaling and stick dampening in many of the important sections.

West Side Story comes out of a jazz tradition of the "swing" era. **Phrasing and "swinging" of the rhythms should be interpreted in this style.**

A note about selecting the proper mallets for this part; large concert halls tend to diminish the attack sound of the vibraphone. **I suggest selecting a set of mallets that are harder than would be comfortable in a more intimate setting.** The harder mallets will produce a sound that will cut through the orchestra and help articulate the more rhythmic sections.

I like to set my pedal height so when it touches the floor the dampening bar just clears the underside of the bars. This avoids overworking your foot and slowing down pedaling. There is no indication of whether the motor should be off or on during this piece. **I have found the motor conflicts with the vibrato of the other instrumentalists.**

Some editions of West Side Story have rehearsal numbers (which are actually the measure numbers and some have only measure numbers, so both are indicated below:

1. <u>Three Measures after Number 15 (m. 17) to Six Measures after Number 25 (m. 30):</u>
    This opening duet with the saxophone is in 6/8 which has a natural "swing" feel. This is also marked "with a jazz feel". **The rhythms are already "swinging" with the triplet effect of the 6/8 time, but certain notes should "stand out" by adding accents to some notes and "ghosting" others.** For instance, in four after Number 15 (m. 18), play the C# less, but bring out the D#. Clear the sound of the other pitches with the pedal before striking the D# to help it stand out. This is also true for the C natural two measures before Number 25 (m. 23). At three measure, after Number 25 (m. 27), Bernstein shows this with a printed accent on the low F. These suggestions are notated below:

2. <u>One Measure before 286 (m. 285):</u>
In this measure, muffle the double stop, C# and E after striking the B and D and while holding the pedal down.

3. <u>Measures 332, 333 and 334:</u>
Hold the pedal down and stick dampen measures 332 and 333. Clear the G with the pedal and stick dampen the C# in measure 334.

4. <u>Number 361 (m. 361):</u>
In this section, pedal according to the slurs indicated in the music.

5. <u>Two before Number 569 (m. 567 and 568):</u>
I suggest using double strokes for the repeated notes in these two measures. This makes it easier to control the rhythm, play accurately, keep it lyrical and follow the conductor. Also, "flutter" the pedal to keep the sound from accumulating and interfering with the *dim. molto.*

6. <u>Number 569 to Three after Number 575 (m. 569 to 577):</u>
This passage is a duet with the solo violin. Listen carefully to the violin to coordinate rhythm and phrasing. **I suggest using stick dampening for the top line.** Consider pedaling between the third and fourth beats in measure 571 if too much sound from the previous A is present. In measures 573 and 574, pedal every note. Also, stick-dampen the C# to D in measure 576.

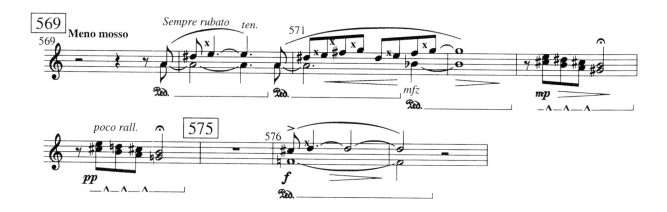

7. Number 581 to Number 656:

Starting at measure 581, there is a long section with confusing rhythmic details. **The first thing to realize is that there is no difference between "swing" 8th notes and "swing" 16th notes.** This long section (m. 581 to m. 607) also has many important notes that need to be emphasized in the jazz style. For instance, in measure 582, the first C is strong and the F# is weak. However, the F# on the third beat is strong while the following C is weak. The next measures repeat this scheme with added Gs which are all weak. **Continue to exaggerate this "strong/weak" crelationship and you will get the character of this entire "Cool" section.**

Use plenty of pedal (arrows) and show the two, three and four-note groups as indicated by the slurs. I also like to use short pedaling (half pedal) for each of the single notes in measures 586 and 587. This creates a better sound than striking an un-pedaled bar too loudly. **Notice, Bernstein has added accents to the strong notes. "Ghost" the unaccented notes to bring this out and create a solid "swing" feel.** Below are two written out examples showing the actual "swing" notation:

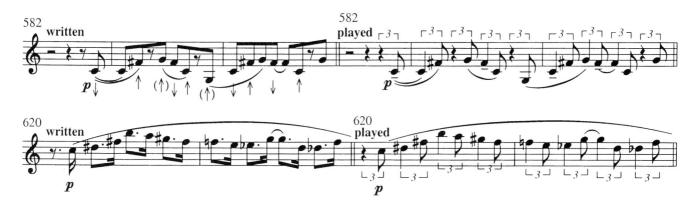

8. Measure 600 to Measure 604:

Pedal and stick dampen as indicated. Delay the *glissando* and keep it on the light side. The grace note should be played as a light, dead-stroke.

9. Measure 615:

The rhythm in measure 615 is incorrect in some editions. Below is the correct rhythm.

10. <u>One Measure before and after Number 625 (m. 624 and 625):</u>

Be particularly careful in measures 624 and 625 that the octave Eb's and E naturals are "swung". This means to place them on the third triplet beats. Also place the 16th note triplets on the third eighth of the triplet. Below is a more accurate notation:

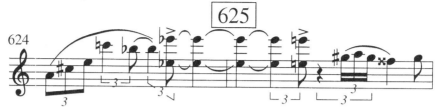

11. <u>Number 620 to Number 635:</u>

The next passage is commonly used for auditions. It contains a wrong note in some editions. The Gb in measure 622 on the third beat should be played as an Ab to match the flute. Notice the pedal markings below and continue to observe the strong and weak notes. Do not overplay the 16th notes in the third beat of measure 622 or the 16th note triplets and dotted 8th and 16th notes that occur three times. These are all just ornaments.

Play the grace notes as dead-strokes as indicated and softer then the accented notes. The part, at Number 620, indicates a *p* dynamic with no further mention until a short *crescendo* to *ff* on a sustaining note (which cannot be done unless a tremolo is added). The *p* dynamic is a solo *espressivo* dynamic and the transition of the passage invites increasing intensity, especially during measure 624 on the octave Eb and then again on the octave F# (m. 628.) Since this note does not exist on the instrument, the bottom F# must be played with the intensity the octave would provide. Measure 633 is incorrect in the part. Below is the correct rhythm. Note the change in rhythm of the D# from a quarter note to an eighth note in measures 626, 627, and 628. This helps emphasize the two E downbeats.

Finally, be sure to phrase the rest of this passage with an accent in the center of all three-note phrase groups.

To Sid Ramin, in friendship

Symphonic Dances from "West Side Story"

Leonard Bernstein

PERCUSSION

82

BERNSTEIN: Symphonic Dances

PERCUSSION

PERCUSSION

BERNSTEIN: Symphonic Dances

BERNSTEIN: Symphonic Dances

About the Author

Jack Van Geem began playing the marimba at age four. He went on to study bassoon, trombone, saxophone, and piano, but in college, decided to major in percussion. He studied with Tony Cirone and Jerome Neff and earned his Master of Arts degree from California State University at Hayward. In 1974, Jack was awarded an Alfred Hertz Traveling Scholarship from the University of California at Berkeley, studying contemporary percussion performance with Cristoph Caskel in Germany. Upon returning to the United States, he became the percussionist for the San Francisco Ballet Orchestra where he remained until winning the Principal Percussion position with the San Francisco Symphony in 1980. Jack is Chairman of Percussion Studies at the San Francisco Conservatory, teaches at the Colburn School of Music in Los Angeles and is the author/composer of three books: *Four Mallet Democracy*, *Rags & Hot Choruses* and *Symphonic Repertoire for Keyboard Percussion*.

Jack has performed under such notable conductors as: Aaron Copland, Freubech De Burgos, Eugene Ormandy, Leonard Slatkin, Kurt Mazur, Edo De Waart, Herbert Blomsted, and Michael Tilson Thomas. Other composer/conductors he has performed with are: Lou Harrison, Steve Reich, John Adams, Charles Wourinin and George Pearl. As a solo marimbist, he performed the American Premiere of *Marimba Spiritual* by Maki Ishi and is a featured artist with the Zeltsman Marimba Festival. Jack Van Geem and Nancy Zeltsman have been performing as a Marimba Duo since 2000 and have released a CD entitled *Pedro and Olga Learn to Dance*. Their repertoire includes a new work by Michael Tilson Thomas entitled *Island Music*. This work was premiered on a New World Symphony concert (Live Webcast) in Carnegie Hall during a San Francisco Symphony concert and, at the 2004 Percussive Arts Society Convention in Louisville, Kentucky.